YOUR KNOWLEDGE HAS VALUE

Bibliographic information published by the German National Library:

The German National Library lists this publication in the National Bibliography; detailed bibliographic data are available on the Internet at http://dnb.dnb.de .

Imprint:

Copyright © 2005 GRIN Verlag, Open Publishing GmbH
Print and binding: Books on Demand GmbH, Norderstedt Germany
ISBN: 9783640461158

This book at GRIN:

http://www.grin.com/en/e-book/137547/service-oriented-architectures-soa

Goetz Viering, Benjamin Müller

Service Oriented Architectures (SOA)

How to find the right Balance between Standardization and Flexibility

GRIN Publishing

GRIN - Your knowledge has value

Since its foundation in 1998, GRIN has specialized in publishing academic texts by students, college teachers and other academics as e-book and printed book. The website www.grin.com is an ideal platform for presenting term papers, final papers, scientific essays, dissertations and specialist books.

Visit us on the internet:

http://www.grin.com/

http://www.facebook.com/grincom

http://www.twitter.com/grin_com

Goetz Viering

Benjamin Müller

European Business School

September 2005

Service Oriented Architectures (SOA)

How to find the right Balance between Standardization and Flexibility

Table of Contents

Index of Graphics

Index of Abbreviations

Abbreviation	Explanation
ASP	Application Service Provider
BPEL	Business Process Execution Language
BPML	Business Process Modeling Language
CAD	Computer Aided Design
CORBA	Common Object Request Broker Architecture
DCOM	Distributed Component Object Model
ERP	Enterprise Resource Planning
ESB	Enterprise Service Bus
HIPAA	Health Insurance Portability and Accountability Act
HP	Hewlett-Packard
HTTP	Hypertext Transfer Protocol
IT	Information and Telecommunication Technology
ISP	Internet Service Provider
KPI	Key Performance Indicator
MS	Microsoft Corporation
OMG	Open Management Group
PRC	People's Republic of China
RMI	Remote Method Invocation
RPC	Remote Procedure Call
SLA	Service Level Agreement
SOA	Service Oriented Architecture
SOAP	Simple Object Access Protocol
SWOT	Strengths, Weaknesses, Opportunities and Threats
UDDI	Universal Description, Discovery and Integration
VoIP	Voice over Internet Protocol
WS	Web Services
WSDL	Web Service Description Language
XML	Extensible Markup Language

1. Introduction

Service oriented architecture (SOA), often enthusiastically emphasized as the future IT infra-structure is currently a big topic in the IT community. IT consultants as well as the software providers are presenting the advantages and possibilities of SOA, but even in the magazines and journals a critical discussion does not seem to occur. The technical features seem to be promising but the advantages from a management perspective remain unclear.

The ideas and principles of SOA are not new but existed for about twenty years. Focusing on the development of IT within this period with its various characteristics and technological developments like the mass production of personal computers, the internet and programming languages uncoupled from the absolute programming it can be clearly stated that from this perspective the concept of SOAs is rather old. Hence, it is interesting to demystify SOA by questioning why it has become such a popular topic during the recent years. Two answers can be given: First of all, even though the concept of service oriented architecture is not new, the technology standard today is for the first time sophisticated enough to make the concept reality and secondly, a lot of companies follow the management trend to restructure their business towards a customer-oriented and process efficient architecture. For those who follow this trend, a SOA offers the flexibility to adapt the IT infrastructure to this new management perspective.

This seminar thesis should provide an introduction into the technology and management possibilities of SOA by describing the status of SOA today, including the advantages and disadvantages from both, technological and management view. Hence, technical and non-technical issues are treated equally. Generic dimensions and strategies should clarify the company specific relevance of SOA and provide a strategic decision-framework. Examples are given and the results are evaluated. Finally, an outlook for possible developments in the future is given.

For the seminar thesis, the assumption is made to focus on companies with an IT infrastruc-ture with a level of complexity and customization requiring constant IT expertise. Both IT and business processes are seen as relevant. For the amortization of both terms it is to be assumed that the business process is in a generic way the disposal of activities whereas the IT process has the supportive status to organize the data flow.

To clearly differentiate between the two, in the following the term IT process is used for describing the IT process and business processes are called business processes.

For this thesis, SOA is the object of examination. The objective is whether the SOA is habile to facilitate or even ameliorate the supportive function of the IT process.

The conceptual design expatiates, next to the introduction four chapters: Fundamentals, Analysis, Future Issues and Conclusion.

In the fundamentals of SOA, as the term already suggests, the basic principles and the derivation of SOA is explained by defining the term as well as the history and technical details.

Both, the historical derivation and technical details are the premises for the contestation. History is important for gaining an understanding of today's status of service oriented architecture and the ability to be able to make future predictions. The technical details explain the function of SOA and are the fundament for the consecutive analysis.

The body of the seminar thesis is the analysis. The analysis is based on a Strengths, Weaknesses, Opportunities and Threats matrix based on Andrews[1] whereby each section covers technical and non-technical occurrences. The result of this analysis should be a comprehensive but general picture of SOAs today. Using this picture, admissible generic dimensions can be deducted which cover the second part of the analysis.

In the second part, a navigator is affiliated from the identified dimensions. This navigator should be a veritable analysis tool for assessing the relevance of SOA. A practical application by companies is designated. Subsequently, four scenarios are presented that on the one hand demonstrate the use of the navigator and on the other hand deduce generic strategies to deal with SOA.

For the outcome of the analysis, best practice examples and statistics provide little insight and are therefore not included in this paper. That is because statistics, like for instance the number of US companies which have already implemented service oriented architecture, do not simplify the decision-making process of a company. On the contrary, best practice examples can simplify the process but the usage is limited to a specific and exemplified industry, e.g. banking. This seminar thesis has a general pretension. Hence, an evaluation of the results of the analysis by an expert in SOA is exposed to proof the generic occurrence.

The future issues present the authors' view of the future development of service oriented architecture. The conclusion summarizes the results of the seminar paper.

2. Fundamentals

After introducing SOAs as the object of examination of this thesis it is important to further clarify this term. As a foundation for the subsequent analysis, this chapter will try to find a definition for SOAs. Afterwards, a section will be dedicated to the historical development of these architectures and their underlying concepts. In the end of this chapter, the technical details of a possible SOA implementation will be given.

---

[1] Cf. ANDREWS (1971), quoted in: FLEISHER, BENSOUSSAN (2003), p. 103.

2.1   Definition

To clarify the object of examination of this paper, this section will try to give a definition what SOA is. When trying to define SOA it is very important to understand that it is not a concrete technical implementation of an idea, but that it describes this idea as an abstraction from all underlying technical questions. The advantage of this is that such an abstraction allows focusing on the relevant concepts on which SOA is based. Picture 1 illustrates the general actors and their relations in a SOA:

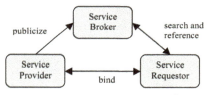

Picture 1: Service Oriented Architecture[2]

In essence, a SOA expresses a software architectural concept that defines the use of services to support the requirements of software users. In a SOA environment, nodes on a network make resources available to other participants in the network as independent services that the participants access in a standardized way.[3] Services are self-contained, stateless business functions which accept one or more requests and return one or more responses through a well-defined, standard interface.[4] Ideally, these business functions are modular, i.e. they provide one bit of very specialized functionality.[5] Another important aspect of services in a SOA is the fact that they are encapsulated.[6] This means that their functionality is contained in an interface layer.

In order to detail out the above definition, two steps will be done. Firstly, the roles of the network nodes will be explained. Secondly, core principles will be identified that constitute a SOA.

The explanation of the components is very straightforward. The Service Requestor[7] is the entity in the network that has a particular need. This can be a calculation program that needs a particular mathematical operation or a software DVD player that requires a special codec. The solution to these problems is offered by the integration of external services, offered by a

---

[2] Cf. DOSTAL et. al. (2005), p. 12.
[3] Cf. WIKIPEDIA (2005).
[4] Cf. WIKIPEDIA (2005).
[5] Cf. GAINES (1977), pp. 16-21.
[6] Cf. DOSTAL et. al. (2005), p. 12; CRAWFORD et. al. (2005), p. 104.
[7] For the purpose of this paper, the terms *requestor* and *client* will be used synonymously.

Service Provider[8]. In order to allow the client to find a proper service, and to be able to compare certain services based on relevant criteria to the user, a central repository that contains this information is integrated into the architecture. This Service Broker[9] holds information comparable to the white/yellow/green pages to facilitate the search and integration of these external services.

While the above roles can also be realized in what is known as object-oriented message exchange architectures, SOA is very literally much more than just the sum of these parts. The reasons for this are the core principles that constitute a SOA. While current literature lists plenty of principles that are regarded to be fundamental[10], 4 core principles can be identified.

- Loose Coupling[11]: This describes the characteristic that the services are generally not dependant on each other. The only dependence is in following the service contracts that are established between a service and a client and that are described in the description at the broker.

- Open Standards[12]: Due to the limited success of older, proprietary implementations of SOAs that often created vendor dependencies and limited the interoperability that is essential for a real distributed architecture, open standards are regarded a very important principle of modern SOAs. This holds especially true when considering the distribution across organizational boundaries and the necessary interoperability.

- Modularity[13]: Service should provide a "granular" functionality. Application-like complexity or business processes are generally realized by composing these granular services. This becomes apparent when considering the statelessness of a service[14], i.e. the independence of any preset condition. Adherence to this principle is necessary to guarantee the dynamic combination of any services, closely related to the loose coupling above. Modularity has already been integrated into early SOA implementations and clearly improves this solution over prior concepts.[15]

- Simplicity[16]: The final core principle is that interfaces created, messages exchanged and protocols used are as simple as possible. The necessity to realize this is also derived from the limited success of past implementations of the SOA concept.

---

[8] For the purpose of this paper, the terms *server* and *service* will be used synonymously.
[9] For the purpose of this paper, the terms *broker* and *repository* will be used synonymously.
[10] Cf. ERL (2005); KOSSMANN, LEYMANN (2004), pp. 118-119.
[11] Cf. ERL (2005).
[12] Cf. DOSTAL et. al. (2005), p. 9.
[13] Cf. BROWN, HAGEL (2003), p. 54.
[14] Cf. WIKIPEDIA (2005).
[15] Cf. ESTREM (2003), p. 513.
[16] Cf. DOSTAL et. al. (2005), p. 9.

2.2 Historic Development

SOA as such is not a new concept. As early as 1999, first implementations of a SOA could be found in the market such as HP's e-Speak. But even before the term SOA appeared, the evolution of what lead to SOAs started in the mid 80's of the last century. Large mainframe computers as a centralized resource executed applications for either local or distant terminals. Over time, the development of more powerful and cheaper micro-processors and more readily available network capacity lead to the creation of Distributed Systems.[17] A problem with this topology was that systems needed to be able to execute programs that were located on a potentially distant resource. Furthermore, data necessary to run this program could be stored on yet another machine. In order to cope with these demands, Remote Procedure Calls (RPCs) were developed and embodied in standards such as the Distributed Computing Environment Standard.

In the mid 90's, Object Oriented and Component Based Programming emerged and started to replace earlier concepts. Within this setting, multiple standards for the realization of distributed systems in an object oriented world started to be realized. Good examples for such systems are Microsoft's Distributed Component Object Model (DCOM)[18], Sun's Remote Method Invocation (Java RMI)[19], or the above mentioned e-Speak of HP. All of these models however have a substantial flaw: they are based on proprietary platforms or programming languages and are hence restricted to a deployment in the respective worlds. As it can be seen later in this paper, one of the major advantages of SOA is the fact that the modular services can be integrated into a business's value chain even across organizational boundaries.[20] When being limited to a MS operating system or the Java language, it becomes virtually impossible to capitalize on this advantage. It cannot be assumed that all businesses involved are running the same platform. Hence, expensive porting would be necessary which often also limits functionality.[21] Furthermore, being limited to any proprietary requirement is often regarded as a hurdle for wide-spread acceptance of a new technology. A good example here is the e-Speak solution that failed to generate any substantial market impact.[22]

A more promising because independent approach was the establishment of the Common Object Request Broker Architecture (CORBA)[23] by the Open Management Group (OMG). CORBA is the first independent architecture to realize a Service Oriented Architecture. The

---

[17] Cf. TANNENBAUM (2003), quoted in: MIHAJLOSKI (2004), p. 10.
[18] Cf. HORSTMANN, KIRTLAND (1997).
[19] Cf. SUN (1997).
[20] See section 3.2, p. 11.
[21] Cf. MIHAJLOSKI (2004), p. 19.
[22] Cf. GISOLFI (2001).
[23] Cf. OMG (2004).

way it works[24] is already very close to the structure of SOAs with Web Services (WS), the most recent development in the area of Service Oriented Architectures. However, the CORBA had and still has some points of critique. The most important one is the inherent complexity of the CORBA. The Carnegie Mellon Software Engineering Institute has analyzed this complexity and concluded that these factors constitute a major challenge to adoption. Especially the fact that SOA implementations of different vendors are still not fully interoperable is pointed out in this analysis.[25]

The next development was the adoption of WS to be used as implementation technology for the concept of SOA. Their both major and yet plain advantage is their inherent simplicity. This simplicity is mainly derived from the use of the Extensible Markup Language (XML)[26]. Through the fact that XML is a generic format for messages, it provides the necessary independence from underlying programming languages and operating system interfaces. Together with the independence of XML from specific vendors, the use of this message format provides a solution to the dependability problem identified above. This concept of XML allows for the realization of the modularity principle and forces developers to use the principle of loose coupling.

The use of WS is the most recent development in the implementation of SOA. But before the analysis of the SWOT-profile of this solution, it is necessary to draw out in more detail how this technology actually works.

2.3 Technical Details

As indicated above SOA is a bare concept, a proposed architecture for an IT landscape. Hence, it is surprising that technical details are offered on something that is explicitly supposed not to be technical. This is the reason why tying the SOA concept to any technical implementation has be critiqued quite recently.[27]

The necessity to do so anyway is derived by the purpose of the analysis of this paper. When trying to aggregate the business and IT context of SOA to derive strategic implications for businesses that are confronted with the potential opportunities of this IT architecture, a tangible technology is more easily assessable than a generic concept.

In the past, as lined out above, such an analysis would have resulted in the examination of a proprietary vendor standard such as RMI or DCOM. The most abstract alternative would have been CORBA. But with WS on the rise as the most promising development in this area, analysis of the technical implementation of SOA with WS seems to be viable and sustainable.

---

[24] Cf. MIHAJLOSKI (2004), pp. 15-18.
[25] Cf. WALLNAU (1997).
[26] Cf. YERGEAU et. al. (2004).
[27] Cf. MACVITTIE (2005), p. 77.

The claims about the future of WS are impressively underlined by the development of market figures for WS. In their report "Web Services Market 2004-2008" the Radicati Group indicates that the market for WS solutions, management, integration and security will rise from USD 950 million in 2004 to USD 6.2 billion on 2008.[28] Given the fact that about 75% of all IT decision makers surveyed by the Yankee Group plan to invest in SOAs in 2005,[29] a considerable share of this growth will come from SOA implementations. The development of WS based SOAs can therefore be considered to be sustainable enough to base our analysis on it.

When explaining how WS work in a SOA it is advisable to extend the triangle with the actors.[30] Especially the transactions between these actors need to be detailed out. Picture 2 provides an overview of the actors, their interactions and details on the transactions.

To describe how the above works, the entire process of creating, publishing, searching, finding, contacting and binding a Service will be examined.

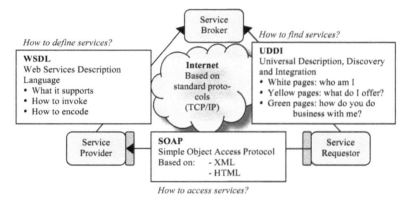

Picture 2: Service Oriented Architecture using Web Services[31]

First of all, the functionality of a Service has to be implemented. When doing so, it does not matter which programming language and/or operating system this functionality is realized in. As described above, the encapsulation of this functionality creates an interface that allows for the exchange of standardized messages rather than specialized program code. In order to create this interface, the Web Service Description Language (WSDL)[32] is used. WSDL is used to describe the Service that is offered. Besides information about the method offered, also input and output parameters are detailed out and the transport protocol in use is specified.

---

[28] Quoted in KERNER (2004a).
[29] Quoted in KERNER (2004b).
[30] See picture 1, p. 3.
[31] In dependence on: MIHAJLOSKI (2004), p. 12.
[32] Cf. CHRISTENSEN et. al. (2001).

This set of data is also called meta-data and can contain much more information than just the examples listed above.[33] These things are new and are also a main differentiator of as WS-based solution compared to the earlier implementations.[34] In the area of SOA, where interoperability is an important topic, the Top-Down Method is generally used for the creation of the WSDL interfaces. Instead of writing the interface for a service first and then generating the interface description (Bottom-Up Method), the description is used to generate the interfaces. This is done because of the possibility that, if the WSDL description is generated based on the provider's interface using one tool, the client side using another tool might not be able to interpret the WSDL correctly.[35] If the WSDL is created by hand, a matching interface can be created on the client side, independent from the tool used.[36]

These interfaces work a bit like the classical machine code example from JAVA. Imagine the following: a service is implemented in JAVA and the client of the requestor is implemented in C++. It is likely that these two cannot communicate directly with one another. To solve this dilemma, the provided service is hidden or encapsulated behind a layer of software that interprets and translates the incoming message. In order to make sure that the service's translator does not need to know all possible incoming languages, an abstract language is used. To allow the client's software to also speak this abstract language, it also needs a translator. These translators are called Skeleton on the service side and Stub on the client side, represented by the dark grey elements in picture 2. As the Stubs are created dynamically when communication with the service is needed, the WSDL is necessary to provide the correct "blueprint" to build the translator.

During communication the abstract language mentioned above is used. This abstract language is called SOAP[37,38]. It is the messaging format used with WS and is based on XML as a data exchange format. Since WS use the everyday internet as the transport platform for the messages exchanged, the HTTP[39] became accepted as the transport protocol for SOAP messages.[40]

But before the exchange of messages can be realized, the client needs to find a service. While the classical peer-to-peer principle, searching of the entire network when the need for a service is realized, certainly is the most dynamic method to do so, response time considerations

---

[33] Cf. KOSCHEL, STARKE (2005), p 18.
[34] Cf. KOSCHEL, STARKE (2005), p. 19.
[35] Cf. MIHAJLOSKI (2004), p. 23.
[36] Cf. MIHAJLOSKI (2004), p. 23.
[37] Cf. GUDGIN et. al. (2003).
[38] Originally SOAP stands for "Simple Object Access Protocol". Since version 1.2 this acronym is no longer in use.
[39] Cf. BERNERS-LEE et. al. (1999).
[40] For a more detailed discussion on how SOAP works cf. WOLTER (2001).

limit the potential of this method. Hence, SOA with WS generally realize an infrastructure based architecture, as seen above. Centralized service repositories, such as the UDDI Business Registry[41] established by IBM, Microsoft, SAP, and NTT-Communications, serve as public, central contact points. As the name of the above database already indicates, Universal Description, Discovery and Integration (UDDI)[42] is very important in this step. It realizes the repository that allows for the search for services and the exchange of information how to contact the service. Optimally the WSDL descriptions are available via an UDDI service. [43]

The general operations of how this architecture works during run time can be divided into two phases: (1) the development phase and (2) the use phase. The first one covers the establishment of the connection between the requestor and the provider. As already indicated above, the requestor contacts the broker using a XML based message to browse the UDDI directory. Once a proper service has been found, the requestor is supplied with the WSDL description of the service and can create the Stub. This concludes the development phase.

During the use phase the client software of the requestor uses the generated stub to generate a XML based SOAP message. It contains the specified inputs and the service request.[44] The Skeleton in the service side receives the message and interprets the content. The input variables are than delivered to the method requested. Afterwards, the operation is reversed and the Skeleton wraps the output of the method in a SOAP message that is delivered to the requestor. Here the Stub interprets the content and delivers the result.

This concludes the second chapter in which the general principles of SOAs were defined, a brief overview over the history and development of these concepts was given, and the most recent implementation using WS was introduced. These insights will be the basis for the subsequent analysis of the SWOT-profile of SOAs in a business context in the next chapter.

3. Analysis

3.1 Methodology

The second chapter has now given a brief description of SOA, its historical development and technical details. With the analysis the exploring part of the seminar paper begins. The analysis is structured in three major parts: the SWOT Analysis, the proposed heuristic framework, and possible scenarios are presented. Finally, the results are evaluated critically. The SWOT Analysis describes the strength, weaknesses, opportunities and threats related to SOA from a

---

[41] Cf. IBM (2005).
[42] Cf. BELLWOOD et. al. (2002).
[43] UDDI as the respective standard is still not as accepted as the other protocols, cf. QUANTZ, WICHMANN (2003), pp. 25-36.
[44] Based on the general structure of a SOAP message other information can also be included. As this level of technical detail is not relevant in the context of this paper, the simple case above is assumed.

non-technical and technical perspective. Using the SWOT Analysis should help to draw a current picture of SOA. Its main purpose is to function as the framework for this picture by classifying the information available in its four distinct categories. The methodology of data gathering for the technical and non-technical issues is on the one hand based on the collection of journals, commercial publications and published interviews. Publications by independent and credible institutions like for example universities or scholarly journals are still rare for the non-technical issues. Interviews with IT experts enhanced this limited scope on the other side. The exploration based on the deducted data provides the strength, weaknesses, opportunities and threats of the SWOT Analysis.

Based on the SWOT Analysis, the proposed framework will be deduced as a second step. The proposed framework should be the heuristic decision tool to classify the need for SOA for a specific company based on qualitative dimensions.

Finally, this framework will be used for four typical scenarios to demonstrate the use of this framework. Furthermore, the scenarios provide the advantages and disadvantages as well as the future development of SOA in a more specific way.

3.2   SWOT Analysis

For this analytical purpose, picture 3 shows the SWOT-matrix of SOA. All the areas of the matrix are divided in technical and non-technical aspects, representing both the business and IT aspects of SOA.

3.2.1 Strengths

Technical

When analyzing the technical strengths of the SOA concept, many of the core principles identified in chapter 2 need to be listed. Foremost this is true for the principle of loose coupling. As described above, this principle allows the services realized in this architecture to be abstracted away from its implementation.[45] When dynamically binding two or more services together, it is absolutely essential to make sure that they all can be combined. In the context of cross-boundary integration of business functions and processes, this technical ability of SOAs with WS is a major advantage of this concept.

Another of the core principles identified were the open standards WS based SOAs are realized with. Compared to the limited success of CORBA, RMI, and DCOM the major advantage here is the elimination of vendor specific implementations. While certain tools for the creation of XML still have vendor specific characteristics, they are all

---

[45] Cf. WILKES (2003).

based on standards that are available to everyone and maintained independently. Not only does this result in the fact that these standards are free, but they also represent a common denominator.

Strengths	Weaknesses
• Loose coupling • Open standards • Standardized interfaces • Chance to keep legacy systems • Modularity • Technical simplicity • Reusability of Services • Greater agility • Reduced reliance • Easy extensibility of business functionality	• Only static Process Modeling possible • Complex monitoring systems necessary • Reliability • Long implementation period • High costs are needed upfront • Skilled development resources are required • Transparency needs to be actively managed
Opportunities	**Threats**
• Dynamic process modeling • Grid computing • Virtualization of resources • Services in Mobile Computing • Unification of IT landscape • Easier hard- and software integration • Global IT Value Chain • More software suppliers • IT differentiation	• Security • Management of business process complexity • Ensure interoperability • Reliable Quality Assurance • Business patch-working • IT architecture becomes area of competition • Top-level support is crucial but difficult • Cultural shift could fail • Sensitivity of system • National regulations

Picture 3: SWOT-Matrix for WS-based SOAs[46]

This in turn helps realizing the independence of underlying standards such as programming language or operating system used. In other words, the standardized XML interfaces encapsulate the service.[47] This encapsulation is of crucial importance for the realization of loose coupling and the integration of services across organizational boundaries.

Another thing this encapsulation makes possible is that businesses can now keep legacy systems when changing their IT. Instead of having to replace working software components, or to rewrite them from scratch in a new system, this software can be encapsulated as a service. The only thing that needs to be done carefully is interface design and implementation. Afterwards the component can be used in the new system with no changes necessary.

Modularity has also been named as one of the core principles for modern SOA.[48] The reason for this being a strength becomes apparent when considering that the develop-

---

[46] The dotted line marks the border between technical and non-technical issues.
[47] Cf. DOSTAL et. al. (2005), p. 20.
[48] Cf. ESTREM (2003), p. 513.

ment and deployment of a small, granular service can be done cheaper and faster[49] when compared to conventional application-based logic. This becomes relevant especially when considering faster time-to-market potential and reduced development costs possible.[50]

Another rather trivial but nevertheless important strength of the WS based realization of SOA is the technical simplicity.[51] Instead of specifications that are 1100 pages long,[52] XML-based WS offer a simple solution that is superior to earlier, proprietary standards. Somers already diagnosed that "different problems now do not have to be solved using different technical solutions [that are often unable to interact with each other], but that they can communicate easily".[53] As far as mere technical know-how is concerned the respective capabilities can be acquired much easier compared to the proprietary implementations of the old object-oriented messaging systems. Hence adaptability of this solution increases over older solutions.

Non-Technical

The strengths of SOA from a non-technical perspective can be clustered in four major areas: Reusability of services, greater agility, reduced reliance and easier extensibility of business functionality.

The reusability of services is a major advantage of service oriented architecture.[54] With the reusability direct and indirect cost savings can be generated.[55] First of all, systems that are already in possession could be used or even used again which would save purchasing or development costs.[56] Another relevant consideration here is the potential for risk reduction through the reuse of proven and mature software.[57]

Secondly, next to the direct costs, indirect cost-savings occur.[58] The employees can use systems they are already used to and hence, no training costs are required, inefficient work-time and mistakes are reduced and less internal customer service from the IT department is required.

In general, redundancy is avoided.

[49] Cf. BROWN, HAGEL (2003), p. 50.
[50] Cf. CRAWFORD et. al. (2005), p. 83.
[51] Cf. DOSTAL et. al. (2005), p. 20.
[52] Cf. OMG (2004).
[53] SOMERS (2005).
[54] Cf. VOELKER (2005), pp. 31-35.
[55] Cf. GRUMAN (2005), p. 63.
[56] Cf. GOLD-BERNSTEIN (2005), p. 2.
[57] Cf. CRAWFORD et. al. (2005), p. 83.
[58] Cf. TAFT (2004), p. 32.

From the management perspective the greater agility SOA offers,[59] has major advantages: As it is possible in a SOA to build the IT infrastructure according to the business processes, the business processes have a simpler structure because they are directly reflected[60] and not build around a non-optimal but required IT infrastructure.[61] The optimization of business processes belongs to the standard tasks on each management layer to reach cost savings and quality improvement through efficiency and control.[62] Hence, an IT infrastructure according to the now possible simpler business processes supports the optimization.[63] Moreover, the combination of the greater agility and the simpler business processes lead to a quicker response time[64] and easier adoption of the business processes to changing external variables and market conditions[65], e.g. new legal issues.

Reliance on one single vendor is today's reality for companies using a standardized ERP system. As stated above, business processes have to be continuously adapted. Additionally, a standardized solution often doesn't offer all the IT function a company requires. In comparison to an ERP solution, SOA offers the ability to easily integrate self-created tools in the existing architecture without continuously employing ERP consultants[66]. The installation, update and maintenance[67] of the single tools are also possible without shutting down the entire system and consequently loss of work-time and quality.[68] The main advantage is that SOA is an alternative to standardized solutions that offers the ability to build the architecture by combining tools of different vendors. That means on the one hand a stronger basis for negotiation but also the possibility to buy products that offer the highest degree of accordance with the demanded functions and tasks. Even though, switching to other IT providers normally generates high costs, SOA facilitates this option in general and more specifically allows new combinations of different tools offered by different vendors. More suppliers with more specialized tools will most likely enter the software market as with the easier integration of single tools in the IT architecture, niche markets have a chance to develop.[69]

---

[59] Cf. KOSCHEL, STARKE (2005), p. 18.
[60] Cf. KHANNA (2005), p. 18.
[61] Cf. MANES (2005), pp. 22-26.
[62] Cf. HOLLIS (2005), p. 40.
[63] Cf. MCKEAN (2005a), p. 8.
[64] Cf. MCKEAN (2005b), p. 4.
[65] Cf. MACVITTIE (2005), p. 77.
[66] Cf. GARVER (2005), pp. 14-15.
[67] Cf. GARVER (2005), pp. 14-15.
[68] Cf. UDELL (2005a), p. 49.
[69] Cf. MANAGEMENT BUSINESS TECHNOLOGY (2005), p. 8; KOSCHEL, STARKE (2005), p. 19.

Hence, companies have more choices, even for specialized tools.[70] However, companies still have the choice to buy from one source if that is the strategic purchasing strategy.

The conversion towards SOA advances the development towards the Global IT Value Chain[71]. The integration of suppliers, manufacturers, wholesaler, vendors and customers into one value chain is an action already in place to reach economies of labor, scale and scope.[72] The large vendors of standardized IT solutions for companies like SAP already try to satisfy the demand by offering these linkages.[73] With an SOA it is possible to integrate different systems of different vendors[74] and hence, economies of labor, scale and scope are quicker to realize.

With its greater agility it is also a major strength of SOA that the business functionality can be more easily extended.[75] That can become for example an important aspect for companies extending or changing their product range by offering new products or services. In- or Outsourcing is also easier with a SOA as parts of the architecture can be integrated or unhinged.[76]

3.2.2 Weaknesses

Technical

A weakness that exists from a technical point of view is the fact that Business Process Modeling is only possible in a static way nowadays. Languages such as the Business Process Execution Language (BPEL)[77] allow for a modeling of business processes using local or distant services, but process chains either have to be very complex to be able to cover each possible case, or they only cover a majority of use cases. No solution currently exists that allows for a dynamic adaptability. How important these things are becomes apparent when considering a sector such as healthcare. If a business process here does not cover rare but possible exceptions in the flow of events, life-threatening situations may result when processes fail.

While these situations need not necessarily kill somebody, failing processes in a highly distributed environment cause a major problem. Consider the following use-case. A Requestor triggers an external service to provide a problem solution. Since the service

---

[70] Cf. CRAWFORT et. al. (2005), p. 3.
[71] The term "Global IT Value Chain" was discussed during the Global IT Value Chain Forum, 19.09.2005 by Prof. Dr. Gerold Riempp.
[72] Cf. BORT (2004), p. 52.
[73] Cf. MANES (2005), pp. 22-26.
[74] Cf. BANERJEE (2005) p. 1.
[75] Cf. MCKEAN (2005c) p. 6.
[76] Cf. BORT (2005) p. 58.
[77] Cf. JURIC (2004).

is encapsulated, the initial Requestor very likely doesn't know whether the service references other services during run-time. If this IT process fails, questions about the source of error and a possible fix arise. Since SOA structures are so highly distributed, or fragmented, error diagnosis is likely to cause major cost in case of defaulting IT processes. This means two things. First of all, "very complex network- and service structure monitoring systems and routines need to be developed".[78] Second, a clear definition of the desired outputs of a service request needs to be ensured. Results need to be checked for probability so that a requesting instance, while knowing nothing about how the result is generated or its exact value, is still able to know when a service failed and when it succeeded. Since external services are some kind of a black box, this is very difficult to realize today. This weakness becomes even more severe when considering legislation such as the Sarbanes-Oxley Act or HIPAA.

A very important IT capability that is also impacted by the change to SOAs is disaster recovery. Only very few experts will be able to remain in a position in which they oversee the entire network. SOA will add yet another dimension to the complex puzzle of downsizing and off-shoring.[79]

The final technical weakness that should be highlighted is a lack of reliability. MacVitties argues that "through the use of the HTTP as transport protocol, the inherently unreliable nature of this stateless protocol also prohibits the use of this implementation with critical transactions".[80] While this may hold true in theory, experience in reality has shown that when using any two proprietary standards, the interoperability is less than when using a common but open standard such as WS and HTTP.[81]

Non-Technical

A major non-technical weakness of SOA is that the value and benefits are only realizable long-term. That is because as an architecture, and not a software program, the conversion is elaborate and costly. In comparison to standardized solutions where architecture is already in place, a new architecture according to the business processes and business needs has to be built which is first of all a business engineering challenge. Next to this challenge, from a programmer's perspective it is also more challenging and time consuming to create the interfaces to new services than enhancing a program with new functions. Hence, the switch from a standardized ERP solution to a

[78] DATZ (2004).
[79] Cf. LUNDQUIST (2005), p. 22.
[80] MACVITTIES (2005), p. 78.
[81] See section 2.2, p. 5.

SOA is the key task as every program has to be connected but furthermore implemented in a meaningful architecture and IT process. Therefore high costs are needed upfront whereas the gain as stated in the strength analysis is only realizable after the successful implementation.

Next to high costs, skilled development resources are required that are in most cases lacking in-house.[82] The job specifications for an SOA expert vary compared to the often employed programmers.[83] Whereas a programmer often builds from scratch[84], the SOA expert has to have the programming knowledge plus a sound understanding of the business as decisions about make or buy, and even more important about where and how to integrate in the business and IT process have to be made.[85] This infrastructure expertise has to be either bought in, for example consultants, or employed in-house. The vocational training of existing programmers into SOA experts is because of the different conceptual approach extensive, too.[86] The need for this expertise at the conversion of SOA is very high whereby some SOA experts highly recommend consultants. However, at a later date, the need is still required for the constant adoption, changes, and problems that appear. Especially the transparency of new structure needs to be actively managed otherwise a loss of ground is most likely because the complexity of the SOA is a much bigger issue than for a standardized solution.

3.2.3 Opportunities

Technical

Many of the opportunities in the future development of SOAs are derived from the weaknesses identified above. A major chance is the dynamic modeling of business processes. Technologies such as Dynamic-BPEL 4 WS may be able to do just that.[87] Then, services can not only be used to model a given process structure of a business today, but they will be able to adapt to changing business processes and logics.[88]

In the past, static software systems were often considered a disabler of organizational change.[89] With the new dynamic SOA however, organically changing businesses are supported in their change by a very flexible IT structure. A good case in point is the healthcare sector already used for illustration above. In a recent article, a hospital's IT

---

[82] Cf. MOSCHELLA (2005), p. 19.
[83] Cf. HALL (2005), p. 42.
[84] Cf. HAVENSTEIN (2005), p. 34.
[85] Cf. UDELL (2005b), p. 30.
[86] Cf. FLOOD (2005), pp. 40-41.
[87] Cf. CAREY (2005).
[88] Cf. appendix 4, p. 41.
[89] Cf. ROBEY et. al. (2000), pp. 144-145.

was described as one of the most complex IT environments. However, success in recent implementations shows that WS based, dynamic SOAs are very well capable of dealing with that.[90]

But these advantages are not only internal. With value chains being disintegrated in recent years, the integration of external services becomes more important. In this context, standardized interfaces of external services allow for a much faster and cheaper integration of external services.[91] This leads to the concept of Business Process Extensibility which allows companies to digitally collaborate with their partners by creating an IT process that crosses organizational boundaries.[92]

A trend that supports the distributed aspects of the SOA concept comes from computing. Over the last couple of years, the concept of grid computing as the architecture for distributed resources became more and more popular.[93] SOA fits very well in such an architecture.[94]

Along with this trend, also the virtualization of resources is an attractive development for many companies. This term describes the trend in which more and more companies only keep a small amount of IT labeled as strategic in-house. Since external services run on distant machines, no or few investment in own IT processing power is needed.[95] Providers of outsourced IT-capacity such as SUN have already tapped into the market of service provisioning.[96] The next step is the development of Application Service Providers which not only host the hardware, but also provide the service. SOA is clearly the technology of choice when realizing such a structure.

Another technical development that goes along with distributed resources is the increased need for mobile computing solutions. With 3G mobile networks on the rise and 4G networks already in development, the bandwidth bottle-neck has been resolved. Now, processing power and memory capacity of the mobile devices become the limiting factors. Since power consumption/battery life and the mere size of the portable terminals limit the potential for a hardware-based solution of these problems, the use of SOA could help resolving this problem.[97] When virtual resources are used

---

[90] Cf. WEBSTER (2005), pp. 26-28.
[91] Cf. DATZ (2004).
[92] Cf. BROWN, CARPENTER (2004), p. 352.
[93] Cf. appendix 4, p. 41.
[94] Cf. ZIMMERMANN et. al. (2003), pp. 548-553.
[95] Cf. BYRD (2005).
[96] Cf. BORT (2004), p. 54.
[97] Cf. ZIMMERMANN et. al. (2003), p. 236.

to take over processing and memory intensive services, the mobile device is reduced to the visualizing front end.[98]

Non-Technical

Assuming that the implementation of SOA will continue and spread in the business environment opportunities for companies can be identified: A unification of the IT landscape is most likely.[99] That seems controversial considering the strength of SOA that the unique business processes can be converted into the IT infrastructure. However, unification hereby means that the IT infrastructure is less antithetic compared to today's situation of either self-provided or bought solutions interconnected with all sorts of interfaces and based on divergent programming standards. Even though, the variety of programming standards will not change, at least the IT architecture with common interface standards will converge. This convergence offers internal as well as external opportunities. Internally, hard- and software integration gets easier[100] and externally, a better digital collaboration in business to business relations is possible. The internal hard- and software integration doesn't only affect the daily expenses but creates real business value when it comes to mergers and acquisition[101] or the outsourcing of entire departments in independent enterprises.[102] Today it is a real challenge for merged companies to generate the promising economies of scale. Often, the restructuring takes years whereby IT integration is one of the big problems. With a possible spread of SOA, mergers could become more attractive, at least from an IT perspective as less post-merger problems can be expected.[103]

A better digital collaboration in the supply value chain does not only affect the cooperation between departments internally but can be extended externally.[104] As mentioned above, a Global IT Value Chain includes the suppliers and customers. This would lead to more economies of scale, scope and labor and hence, large interconnected trading conglomerates[105], comparable to today's automotive industry with just-in-time production and delivery, as well as optimization along the whole supply value chain is possible.

---

[98] Cf. appendix 4, p. 41.
[99] Cf. MCKEAN (2005d), p. 8.
[100] Cf. ALSOP (2005), p. 35.
[101] Cf. NATIONAL MORTGAGE NEWS (2004), p. 6.
[102] Cf. SILVER (2005), p. 26-30.
[103] Cf. NATIONAL MORTGAGE NEWS (2004), p. 6.
[104] Cf. MACVITTIE (2005).
[105] Cf. ZEICHICK (2005), p. 37.

As niche players have an easier access into the business to business area with special-ized offerings, a service-trading network will arise with hosts as new market players providing accumulations of services.[106] This development is most likely as communi-cation costs between the service creator and service user would otherwise increase enormously. This development would question the concept of IT service ownership[107] and a customizability of services would be possible. These new possibilities make an IT differentiation possible which could be used as competitive advantages at least for the first mover through efficiency, service improvements and cost savings.[108]

3.2.4 Threats

Technical

A point that is considered a major threat for the further successful development of SOA is Security. As easy as external solutions are integrated, as easy intruders could use this possibility to jeopardize a company's IT infrastructure. This is especially true when considering the HTTP-based XML solutions of about 90% of all SOA imple-mentations today. Manifold solutions to these problems have already been suggested and are currently discussed in the literature.[109]

Other than in the case of the technical simplicity,[110] simplicity in a business context is not necessarily given with this architecture. While older technical solutions were either based on legacy solution created in house with own know-how and resources or ven-dor based standard IT processes, SOA is likely to cause complexity in the administra-tion of business processes and the underlying service chains. As these are crossing or-ganizational boundaries, seeing the big picture becomes very difficult. But not only the administration of the networks will be challenging, also the business implications such a solution has, are severe.

During the analysis of the strengths of SOA the interoperability was recognized as a major point. However, current implementation of tools to work with WS still allow for the freedom of interpretation. Not all WS realizations are necessarily interoperable. However, this problem has been recognized by the WS community and with the estab-lishment of the WS-Interoperability initiative considerable results have already been achieved towards a truly and reliably interoperable WS world.[111]

---

[106] Cf. BAER (2005), p. 41.
[107] Cf. YAGER (2004), p. 50.
[108] Cf. FLOOD (2005), pp. 40-41.
[109] Cf. DOSTAL et. al. (2005), pp. 163-195; CARLSON, HIMLER (2005), pp. 31-33.
[110] See subsection 3.2.1, p. 11.
[111] Cf. DOSTAL et. al. (2005), pp. 40-41.

A final threat that makes SOA dangerous is the potential to allow businesses to fix problems by patch-working. This means instead of understanding why a certain (legacy) service constantly produces wrong results, it is simply wrapped in another layer of interfacing technology. This not only limits organizational learning, but also causes opaque IT systems. In other words businesses may tend to constantly renew solutions whereby the core is way outdated instead of replacing them.

Non-Technical

Even though, a competitive advantage with the implementation of the SOA could be gained, competitors will most likely use the same opportunities to overhaul. Hence, the IT architecture becomes a relevant area of competition.

Next to this new field of competition, especially the implementation is, as already stated, costly, elaborate, and interminable. Top-level support is crucial for the success of the whole implementation[112] as an early abruption would lead to a total failure without any benefits. Short-term oriented management goals focused on satisfying the shareholder value could easily abrupt the implementation, especially a change in top-management. The cultural shift in the IT department is important but difficult.[113] Without reaching a cultural shift, the successful implementation will fail as SOA requires development discipline and technical attributes have to be clearly defined at the beginning. Reusable services have to be identified, too. That is not likely to occur without the expertise and motivation of the employees. Organizational learning is vital but employees are often unwilling to do so.

If the implementation was successful, the SOA is far from being a self-running system. The infrastructure needs to be managed and maintaining SOA also requires development discipline. The reporting requirements are difficult to manage[114] and setting up meaningful IT KPIs for performance measurement is a challenging task[115]. Particularly, in companies using external services from hosts as service deliverers and not a software platform like FuegoBPM.[116]

As SOAs may increase system complexity[117], dependency on internal or external key SOA experts with an understanding of the IT architecture increases, too.

---

[112] Cf. COMMUNICATIONS NEWS (2005), pp. 6-8.
[113] Cf. MANES (2005), pp. 22-26.
[114] Cf. SMITH (2005), p. 12.
[115] Cf. KENDLER (2005), pp. 40-41.
[116] Cf. KM World (2005), p. 30.
[117] Cf. MOSCHELLA (2005), p. 18.

A mutual integration in the form of a Global IT Value Chain is also limited by different national regulations[118] concerning data protection and data flow. Different regulations are already in place as for example between the US and Europe or the PRC with its highly regulated internet use.[119] The Global IT Value Chain as well as the use of service hosts can create many entries and exits in the IT architecture[120]. With more open slots it is increasingly difficult to protect the system against internet crime like for example industrial espionage.[121]

3.3 Summary of Analysis

The SWOT-profile of SOA analyzed above leads to the discovery of four main issues: (1) strategic considerations of companies when deciding whether to adopt SOA or not, (2) process characteristics of the business processes they target to support with such an architecture, (3) cultural variables within their company, and (4) the capital requirements that such a solution would cause. For each of these, respective strengths, weaknesses, opportunities, and threats will be identified to aggregate our results into a framework to analyze a company's position in terms of SOA "readiness".

Since strategy is widely considered one of the most important determinants of economic success, a SOA needs to be checked for its implications on a business's strategy. Within this area, especially the strategic relevance of the impacted business processes needs to be evaluated. Considerations like potential externalization and scalability are important here. On top of that, also the IT capabilities in general and SOA in particular need to be examined. Besides the current IT strategy, also the desired degree of internalization of an implementation needs to be considered.

The IT process characteristics we have identified encompass questions about IT process dependability, variability, and complexity. The first looks into availability and reliability issues while linking this area with the strategic considerations above. The second reflects the discussion about the loose coupling characteristic of SOA and the resulting interoperability when using WS. The final issue on IT process complexity is based on structural and dimensional complexity. The first one refers to the structure of the IT processes to be conducted in a SOA where the loose coupling and dynamic modeling become interesting. The latter refers to whether IT processes are purely internal, external, or a combination of both.

Within the area of cultural variables a specific analysis of the IT department as well as a holistic view on the entire company are proposed. For the IT department, the role that it cur-

---

[118] Cf. COFFEE (2005), p. D6.
[119] Cf. LUNDQUIST (2005), p. 22.
[120] Cf. INFOWORLD(2005), p. 59.
[121] Cf. TILLER (2005), p. 3.

rently plays within its organization needs to be examined. When focusing on the entire organization, especially the organizational learning patterns[122] have to be examined.

The final area that needs to be addressed is the capital connected to SOA implementations. While the revenues are important to understand the need of a company in terms of desired cost structure, also the expected realization of results needs to be analyzed.

3.4   Proposed Framework

When using the main areas and their dimensions, it becomes obvious that companies need to asses their individual situation on all of the dimensions above. Therefore we propose the SOA Navigator as a strategic tool for companies facing the decision to adapt a SOA.

The navigator uses the main areas as a first structural level to grasp the complexity of the decision to tap into SOA. Based on the summary of the SWOT analysis in section 3.3, which assigned topics to the four main areas, these topics were used to design qualitative dimensions of assessment. Picture 4 shows the resulting structure of the Navigator with its dimensions:

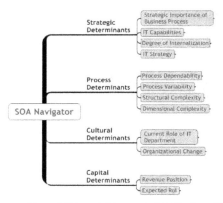

Picture 4: Schematic View on the SOA Navigator[123]

When using the navigator, businesses will use these dimensions to determine their qualitative value in each of them. For each of the dimensions a 5-point scale is proposed. This is done to give companies flexibility when assessing their situation.[124]

---

[122] Cf. ROBEY et. al. (2000), pp. 129-133.
[123] For a complete picture of the SOA Navigator including all qualitative values per dimension please refer to appendix 1, p. 34.
[124] For a detailed description of all dimensions and values please refer to appendix 2, p. 35.

This assessment is then used to be visualized in a spider-web graph. The resulting profile is used to determine whether SOA is an interesting option for the business and in which way this option should be realized.

In order to detail out the methodology proposed, the following subsection will conduct a scenario analysis for four hypothetical companies.

4. Scenario Analysis

This section will use four companies to demonstrate the application of the SOA Navigator to a business setting. The resulting profiles of the four companies will be used to recommend generic strategies that these companies should use when considering SOAs.

4.1   Scenario "Internal Solution"

A possible example that could serve as a case in point here is an international airline. Market conditions for these companies have been quite adverse recently and fierce competition forced many of them to re-invent their business models. In many cases, IT played a major role in the transformation.

The primary business processes of this airline, e.g. baggage handling or flight scheduling, are highly relevant to the scenario since they use IT directly. IT capabilities have to be high as they enabled the IT change mentioned above. Hence, to ensure individuality of a solution, the company will use this expertise to realize an internal solution. To support the differentiation focus of the company, IT strategy is also highly innovation driven.

Since the core processes of the airline are impacted, a very high dependency is needed. The process variability in general is comparably high because many external factors have to be accounted for, e.g. weather. On top of that, modern airport environments are a landscape of many external partners such as catering service, flight control and ground services. Complex processes with many interfaces result. As already stated, this directly affects the IT processes.

With the fragmented character of the modern value chain the IT department is found to play a more integrating role, while dynamic markets in the recent past forced the company to adapt a dynamic organizational learning pattern.

To complete the picture, volatile fuel prices in aviation, varying demand due to external shocks and other factors result in an unstable revenue position. In order to cope with these challenges, a long-term solution needs to be found.

The scenario described above resulted in a navigator profile[125] that implies a highly capable company that needs an agile IT solution to supports business dynamics. An external provider can hardly fulfill this challenging task because of the company's dimension and complexity of

---

[125] See appendix 3: Navigator Profile of Scenario "Internal Solution", p. 39.

the IT processes. Hence, an SOA Navigator Profile like this indicates the necessity and possibility of an internal solution. This does not only encompass the mere creation and provisioning of services, but also the build-up and management of the infrastructure needed.

4.2   Scenario "Host-based Solution"

This scenario will be illustrated using a large private healthcare center as an example. Focus of IT systems here tends to be more efficiency driven since they support secondary business processes like administering data transfer or activity coordination. IT capabilities of the institution are existent, but especially in the area of SOA far from sufficient. Hence, a higher degree of externalization is needed. In line with the efficiency focus above, today's IT strategy is more cost than innovation oriented.

As far as business processes are concerned, highly dependable IT processes are needed, too. This becomes obvious when considering the fact that in case of failure human life may be endangered. Since emergencies and unpredictable exceptions are likely to occur, the IT process variability is very high in this context. This also implies a higher degree of IT process complexity. Since emergency medical services and after-stay care needs to be coordinated, multidimensional IT processes are executed.

Based on this insight, integration is a major part of the tasks of the IT department. No significant learning pattern could be identified and hence, a neutral position on this axis is assumed.

The revenue position of the institution is volatile based on the unpredictability of demand. To adapt to this, very scalable IT will result in variable cost structures.

All the descriptions above can be aggregated and visualized into a navigator profile for this company.[126] This profile implies that the internal capabilities in this case are limited and lower strategic importance does not require an internalization of these capabilities. Hence, the internal solution introduced above is not needed here. However, the dynamic business and IT processes demand for a both dynamic and scalable solution. To capitalize on these advantages, the healthcare institution is likely to need an external partner that takes over the administration of the infrastructure. The creation and provisioning of services is not impacted by this recommendation. Such an external partner could act as a "Host", providing services on a pay-per-use base, e.g. realized in the form of a SLA. While not meaning that the Host physically hosts all services needed, it is hosting the coordination of the internal needs and the external services. Since it knows the market for required services very well, it can provide redundancy easily and ensure the needed dependability. By doing so, the Host will also function as a liability buffer for the services.

---

[126] See appendix 3: Navigator Profile of Scenario "Host-based Solution", p. 39.

Another tempting characteristic of the Host-based solution is that it will be the only creditor for the institution, Instead of having to deal with each external Service Provider individually, the Host takes over this responsibility.[127]

4.3 Scenario "Vendor-based Solution"

This Scenario will describe the dimensions of a classical Internet Service Provider as the sample company. For the ISP the IT process is strategically highly important as the service, billing and the actual product are totally dependent on the IT process. As a participant of the IT industry it can be assumed that IT capabilities are abound and consequently the degree of internalization is high. The IT strategy is focused on innovation because less differentiation potential in pricing is possible and only innovation provides competitive advantage.

The IT process variability is rather limited as the provisioning of the accessibility is a very stable process. While the structural complexity shows no significant implications, the low dimensional complexity shows the small integration of external value partners into the IT processes. Dependability of this process is important, however, minor insufficiencies can be tolerated.

In terms of cultur the IT department occasionally integrates while development is still re-garded a major task. A dynamic learning pattern cannot be observed.

Since stable contracts with its customers provide the ISP with likewise stable revenues that are combined with the high strategic value, a long-term horizon for the realization of the result is regarded as a realistic scenario here. Once more, this diagnosis was used to create a navigator profile for this case.[128]

The major implications for realization strategy are derived from the combination of the di-mensions that is characterized by the profile above. While high values in the strategic dimen-sion show that internal implementation would be good, the lower ones in the process dimen-sions show that for example a modularized ERP system would be sufficiently sophisticated to serve the requirements of the example company. Hence, a profile like the above recommends a highly customizable product that was created by an external vendor and implementation is generally supported by an intermediary.

Products that are applicable here are not classical ERP solutions, but new developments, generally summarized under the term Enterprise Service Bus (ESB)[129]. Further discussion of the concept and its implications is covered in the literature.

---

[127] The implications this has on the business relationship are manifold, e.g. better negotiating position through higher billing volume when service adaptation is needed or when trying to fix problems.
[128] See appendix 3: Navigator Profile of Scenario "Vendor-based Solution", p. 40.
[129] Cf. PASLEY (2005), pp. 24-29.

4.4 Scenario "Off-the-shelf Solution"

This solution can be applied mainly to small and medium enterprises. Hence, a typical production company from the German "Mittelstand" has been chosen as the illustrating example here.

The manufacturing processes are vital for the company's success. While production scheduling and related tasks supporting the manufacturing are based on IT, they normally are not the focus of the company. Hence, internal IT capabilities exist, but only in a limited way. This results in a low degree of internalization if major implementation projects are undertaken. Since IT is not likely to be a primary source of competitive advantage, cost is favored over innovation.

The business processes that are modeled in IT systems are generally found to be stable over time and limited in their structural complexity. While external partners exist in some areas, e.g. suppliers, their number and the missing IT interfaces with them justify lower values in the dimensional complexity area. Dependability of business processes is vital, but IT default cannot cause major problems in the short run.

In line with the IT profile so far, the role of the IT department is mainly driven by development tasks. Organizational change capabilities are existent but were not found to have significant effects in this scenario.

The revenue position of the company is rather stable, while still being exposed to economic fluctuations. IT projects in this context are generally used to react to current problems or to keep pace with the industry standard. Because of that, a short- to mid-term realization of the result is appreciated.

With all this a navigator profile for this company[130] implies the following: Since IT does not play a major part in the operations of this company, the major cultural and technological implications of a SOA implementation are considered to be far beyond the scope of interest of such a company. Even the large Middleware products or Host-based solutions are over sized since neither the agility of SOA is needed nor strategic justifications for the investment of financial and human resources exist.

4.5 Summary

The above scenarios have illustrated the use of the SOA Navigator and the exemplary interpretation of the results of this application. Generally speaking, the more area is covered in the SOA Navigator Profile, the more suitable SOA based IT solutions become. On top of that, an entirely covered area suggests an internal realization of this opportunity. In-house capabilities

---

[130] See appendix 3: Navigator Profile of Scenario "Off-the-shelf Solution", p. 40.

are needed to fully capitalize on the SOA potential. If the Profile shows significant concentration in any one of the general areas or dimensions, hybrid strategies are needed. These are tempting because they use external expertise to complement the company's Profile, hence, overcoming weaknesses and sources of a potential implementation failure. If only a small part of the Profile is covered, SOA was found to be unattractive for companies.

However, it needs to be lined out that results need to be interpreted by companies individually. While the four strategies lined out above can be looked at as four generic ones to tap into SOA, the possibility for companies to adapt this new IT architecture are as individual as the companies themselves. Nevertheless, the SOA Navigator provides a basic tool to structure the problematic areas important in regard to SOA.

5. Evaluation of Results

The final section is a critical evaluation of the results. To conduct this evaluation, external academic knowledge and practitioners' advice were used. A detailed interview about the analysis, the resulting framework, and its application was done.

The feedback on the analysis showed that the division in technical and non technical issues characterizes the main areas of discussion today. Examination of the SWOT profile in the two categories revealed that the topics covered are relevant. However, the degree of actuality and completeness is difficult to assess since rapid changes and steady developments still take place. Each issue can be examined in greater detail.

As far as the analysis is concerned, the not entirely efficient character of the XML-based messages was pointed out as an additional weakness. However, the possibility to be able to read these messages as a human is reducing the severity of this weakness.

Additional opportunities were seen in the area of the semantic development of web services. Also the possibility to achieve quality improvements using Services was mentioned. On top of that, the potential of SOA to virtualize human interaction was described.

Aside from opportunities, also additional threats were identified. While stating that security issues are likely not to be an issue of SOA per se, the security weaknesses of using the internet in a SOA were pointed out. Likewise the fixes to those problems are likely to come from the internet community and not from further SOA development.

On the management side, the described unification of the IT landscape will be difficult in reality. It still can simplify mergers and acquisitions. The main unification potential was seen within a firm, relating to the different entities herein.

Points mentioned relating to weaknesses and threats were technical KPIs that are likely to be developed in the near future. Therefore they will no longer be a critical weakness. As far as the difficult cultural shift from development to integration in the IT department is concerned, the interview indicated that the demand for this role is likely to produce respective educational offers.

However, the analysis was found to grasp the relevant problem domains and hence, the development of the framework based on this analysis produces a sound result.

From an information technology point of view, the resulting framework was found to lack a sufficient description of IT process quality. Since quality is inferred in the "Expected RoI" dimension, this problem was found to be non-critical.

Based on the interview, all scenarios were found to be applicable. Nevertheless, further remarks were made. While the current developments in the airline sector seem to confirm the scenario described, two main points were critiqued. First, while the ISP was found to be a fitting example, it has to be noted that the "classical" ISP is a vanishing business model. Today's ISPs try to earn their revenues by providing value-added services, a context in which the SOA considerations have to be reevaluated. Second, the production company was found to also have demand for SOAs, but only in separate modules, e.g. CAD in Research and Development. The ERP product world is not impacted by these considerations.

According to the interviewee, the approach can be applied to practical settings.

6. Future Issues

In the recent history of SOA, the use of relatively simply and platform independent Web Services was crucial for the adoption of the architecture in the business world. In order to foster its success, several issues need to be addressed in the near future. Also the conducted interview pointed towards interesting developments in terms of SOA.

One of the most important ones certainly is the development of technologies that are able to dynamically generate and execute process chains. While the static modeling of these is done by technologies such as BPEL 4 WS or BPML, dynamic concepts are crucial to map dynamic business processes in a distributed IT landscape.[131]

Along with the development of the modeling capabilities, also underlying technical issues will evolve further. While Web Services already show a successful history as SOA implementation technology, further development is expected. After a consolidation of standards which concludes the phase of development of extended standards, the coming development is depicted in Dostal et. al.'s Web Services Waves.[132] Based hereon, semantic specifications are the next step to come.

---

[131] See discussion in subsection 3.2.3, p. 17; cf. CAREY (2005).
[132] Cf. DOSTAL et. al. (2005), p.43.

However, the biggest and most promising step will be the development of a market for (Web) Services.[133] Within this relatively wide topic, many smaller issues need to be examined. The most important are that companies such as ASPs, broker of the repositories and the host's role described in the generic strategies will evolve to act as market-maker, making transactions more transparent and acting as intermediaries. Moreover, companies will be confronted with the question in which way they also want their internal services to be provided on external markets and vice versa.[134] A development that could work in the area of security organizationally speaking is the establishment of independent security and certification agencies. These allow for Quality Assurance of external services and reliable identity checking of Providers and Requestors. Businesses need to be able to rely on a distant service to deliver the results it is promising within the parameters specified. Feedback mechanisms in case of problems need to be found to be able to react in case of default and to ease disaster recovery.

Along with the technical and external developments, also internal changes need to be faced. For example, developers will have to shift their development paradigm. The reason for this was identified by Havenstein. Instead of developing one-off solutions that developers don't have to work with once they successfully crossed testing and deployment, now "already deployed pieces of software have to be constantly re-engineered".[135] Orientation in a functionality framework will become the most important capability and the integration of these software pieces the qualification of future IT experts. This applies not only to internal services, but also to changes in process chains involving external services.

All of the above areas are considered crucial to a successful further development of SOAs, whether based on WS or not.

7. Conclusion

This seminar thesis has shown the relevancy of SOA in the near future. While not being a new concept, recent improvements over older implementations of SOA, e.g. CORBA, made it a hot topic again. One of these developments certainly is the use of WS that allow a very close realization of this architecture. The use of WS therefore made the application of SOA to more distributed business processes more realistic than ever before. Based on this, the philosophy behind SOA may well be capable of becoming the next big paradigm in Software Engineering and Development after object orientation. Today it is not predictable whether this shift will also impact the modern business or not. However the authors believe that there is a realistic chance that such impacts will happen in the near- to mid-term future. In order to prepare itself

---

[133] Cf. BORT (2004), p. 54.
[134] Cf. DOSTAL et. al. (2005), pp. 127-128.
[135] HAVENSTEIN (2005), p.35.

to face potential challenges and to capitalize on upcoming opportunities, businesses are advised to understand their current position in the SOA world.

To be able to do so, a holistic approach covering the technical and management-oriented perspective of this problem domain is needed. Such an approach needs to be based on an analysis of the current situation. To support businesses in their task to prepare themselves, this paper used such an analysis to develop the SOA Navigator. This framework will help companies of all industries to identify the relevant dimensions and to asses their position hereon. The resulting profile will give these companies a first impression of their perspectives on a potential adaptation of SOA.

The topic will remain an interesting area. Both, scientific and business community will produce further developments in the next years. Possible directions of these were provided in the outlook chapter of the paper as well as in the interview conducted.

The authors hope that the SOA Navigator in its simplicity is able to assist companies by providing a wholesome approach to this new topic, even though further analysis will have to be conducted in each company to make sure that all the envisioned improvements can actually be realized.

Appendices

Appendix 1: The SOA Navigator

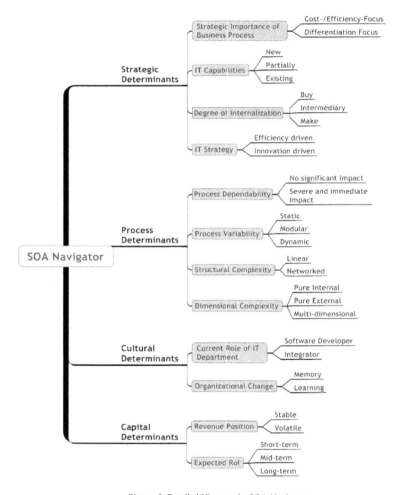

Picture 5: Detailed View on the SOA Navigator

Appendix 2: Further Details on Navigator Dimensions

The SOA Navigator provides the framework for companies to decide whether the implementation of SOA makes sense and if so, how the implementation should take place. Hereby it is important to understand that the SOA Navigator is an As-Is-Analysis and only the combined profile of all 12 dimensions allows for strategic implications. The general application of the Navigator targets each business process individually. Afterwards, the individual results can be aggregated to a holistic company view.

The definition of the dimensions is important for the correct classification of the enterprise attributes but it is also vital for the consistency and understanding of the SOA Navigator. Hence, in the following, each dimension is defined.

Strategic Determinants:

For this dimension it is essential to understand that the object of analysis are the business processes of an enterprise.

- Strategic Importance of Business Functionality:

1	2	3	4	5
Cost-/ Efficiency Focus	...	...	...	Differentiation Focus

The Strategic importance of the process questions whether the business process is the source of differentiation and hence, is the core value creation process. Considerations like whether it is strategically viable to externalized this functionality or the transaction count of this functionality are covered.

- IT Capabilities

1	2	3	4	5
New	...	Partially	...	Existing

The IT Capabilities position describes the degree of internal IT knowledge and skills available to be used to successfully deal with IT change and new architecture implementation.

- Degree of Internalization

1	2	3	4	5
Buy	...	Intermediary	...	Make

If the company would decide for an implementation project in the context of SOAs today it has to consider whether to choose an external product of not and how to implement it.

- IT Strategy

1	2	3	4	5
Efficiency driven	...	...	...	Innovation driven

Hereby it has to be considered whether today's IT strategy is more efficiency or innovation driven. This is an important dimension as it is difficult to be innovative without an innovative culture and a swap from a more efficient to an innovative culture takes time.

Process Determinants:

Other than focusing on business processes, these dimensions examine the IT process that is used to support the business process. These dimensions mainly reflect the resulting considerations of the technical issues connected with SOAs.

- Process Dependability

1	2	3	4	5
No significant impact	...	...	...	Severe/Immediate impact

The process dependability accounts for the redundancy and scalability considerations. The key focus is the degree of consequence in case of a default of the services. It is clear that a default in most cases has consequences. However, it makes a difference whether a company could live with this default a week or only a few hours without being in serious struggle.

- Process Variability

1	2	3	4	5
Static	...	Customizable	...	Dynamic

Process Variability questions how variable the IT processes are today. These can be either more static or more variable. It has to be noted that static means that the entire

IT process in all its components doesn't change. Customizable processes have modules that can be exchanged, but each of the modules has to be executed fully. The dynamic process is also combined of modules, but these modules can be halted and resumed during run-time.[136]

- Structural Complexity

1	2	3	4	5
Linear	...	...	...	Networked

Here, a complex structure or linear structure of the process is examined. Linear structure describes basic and standardized procedures whereas the complex structure is more multilayered, unique and elaborate.

- Dimensional Complexity

1	2	3	4	5
Pure internal	...	Pure external	...	Multi-Dimensional

The dimensional complexity describes the degree of integration along the value chain. Are the relevant activities in-house only or purely external or do both dimensions have to be integrated.

Culture Determinants:

This area covers the cultural variables that would impact a SOA implementation. It covers both a specialized view on a company's IT department and a holistic approach towards the entire company:

- Current role of IT department

1	2	3	4	5
Software Developer	...	...	...	Integrator

Today's skills and orientation are described in the current role of IT department. The two extremes are either a majority of programmers and adapters or SOA experts as architecture integrators and business analysts.

---

[136] This implies technical capabilities that allow for state-full services.

- Organizational Change

1	2	3	4	5
Memory	...	...	...	Learning

If the organizational change pattern is dominated by organizational memory the change in IT architecture and philosophy is likely to be more difficult than if compared to an organization where dynamic change and organic development are the major organizational change pattern.

Capital Determinants:

To cover the financial side of an SOA project, the following financial considerations are also covered. Individual decisions, however, have to be backed by a detailed investment calculation.

- Revenue Position

1	2	3	4	5
Stable	...	...	...	Volatile

The revenue position describes the degree of necessity to which variable cost structure is needed. With a volatile revenue position, variable costs are needed to adjust IT costs in comparison to higher IT fix costs with a more standardized solution.

- Expected ROI

1	2	3	4	5
Short-term	...	Mid-term	...	Long-term

For the implementation of SOA, a stable flow of revenues for financing is crucial. Therefore it has to be examined when the new solution is supposed to pay off and when the organization needs the benefits that are expected. Another thing covered here are considerations about improved process quality since they influence the economic value gained once a solution is implemented.

Appendix 3: Navigator Profiles of Scenarios

Scenario 1: "Internal Solution"

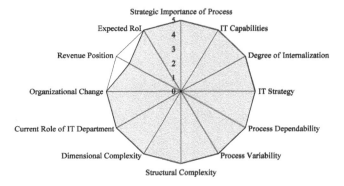

Picture 6: Navigator Profile of Scenario "Internal Solution"

Scenario 2: "Host-based Solution"

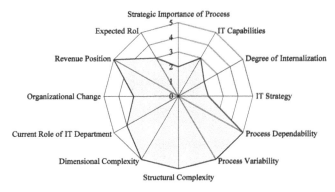

Picture 7: Navigator Profile of Scenario "Host-based Solution"

Scenario 3: "Vendor-based Solution"

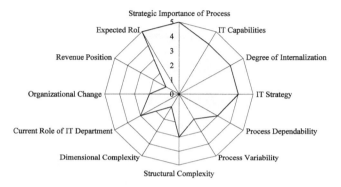

Picture 8: Navigator Profile of Scenario "Vendor-based Solution"

Scenario 4: "Off-the-shelf Solution"

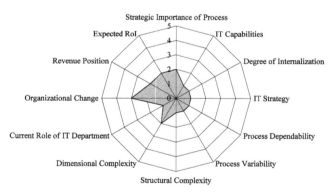

Picture 9: Navigator Profile of Scenario "Off-the-shelf Solution"

References

ALSOP, Joe (2005): Driving Progress, in: eWeek, June 2005, Vol. 22, Iss. 25, p. 35.

ANDREWS, K. (1971): The concept of corporate strategy, 3. Edition, Homewood.

BAER, Tony (2005): Brewing a new kind of connection, in: Manufacturing Business Technology, January 2005, Vol. 23, Iss. 1, pp. 40-42.

BANERJEE, Akash (2005): The Case for SOA, in: Byte.com, July 2005, p. 1.

BELLWOOD, Tom / CLÉMENT, Luc / EHNEBUSKE, David / HATLEY, Andrew / HONDO, Maryann / HUSBAND, Yin Leng / JANUSZEWSKI, Karsten / LEE, Sam / MCKEE, Barbara / MUNTER, Joel / von RIEGEN, Claus (2002): UDDI Version 3.0 – UDDI Spec Technical Committee Specification, http://uddi.org/pubs/uddi-v3.00-published-20020719.htm, published: 19.07.2002, downloaded: 16.09.2005.

BERNERS-LEE, T. / FIELDING, R. / FRYSTYK, H. / GETTYS, J. / LEACH, P. / MASINTER, L. / MOGUL, J. (1999): Hypertext Transfer Protocol – HTTP 1.1, http://www.w3.org/Protocols/rfc2616/rfc2616.txt, published: 06.1999, downloaded: 18.09.2005.

BORT, Julie (2004): The 'Uncertainty Principle', in: Network World, November 2004, Vol. 21, Iss. 46, pp. 51-54.

BORT, Julie (2005): You in an SOA world, in: Network World, July 2005, Vol. 22, Iss. 29, pp. 58-60.

BROWN, John Seely / HAGEL III, John (2003): Flexible IT, better strategy, in: McKinsey Quarterly, 2003, Iss. 4, pp. 50-60.

BROWN, George / CARPENTER, Robert (2004): Successful Application of the Service-Oriented Architecture Across the Enterprise and Beyond, in: Intel Technology Journal, 2004, Vol. 8, Iss. 4, pp. 345-359.

BYRD, Jim (2005): Grid and Your SOA Strategy, http://www.virtual-strategy.com/article/articleview/1159/1/2, published: 09.02.2005, downloaded: 19.09.2005.

CAREY, Sean (2005): Part 3: Making BPEL Processes Dynamic, http://www.oracle.com/technology/pub/articles/bpel_cookbook/carey.html, published: 2005 (year of copyright), downloaded: 19.09.2005.

CARLSON, Brent / HIMLER, Alan (2005): Turning Application Security Inside Out: Security for Service-Oriented Architectures (SOAs), in: Information Systems Security, September/October 2005, Vol. 14, Iss. 4, pp. 27-35.

CHRISTENSEN, Erik / CURBERA, Francisco / MEREDITH, Gred / WEERAWARANA, Sanjiva (2001): Web Services Description Language (WSDL) 1.1, http://www.w3.org/TR/wsdl, published: 15.03.2001, downloaded: 16.09.2005.

COMMUNICATIONS NEWS (2005): Buyers, vendors not on same page, in: Communications News, July 2005, Vol. 42, Iss. 7, pp. 6-8.

COFFEE, Peter (2005): SOA demands new way of thinking, in: eWeek, April 2005, Vol. 22, Iss. 16, pp. D6-D7.

CRAWFORD, C. H. / BATE, G. P. / CHERBAKOV, L. / HOLLEY, K. / TSOCANOS, C. (2005): Toward an on-demand service-oriented architecture, in: IBM Systems Journal, 2005, Vol. 44, Iss. 1, pp. 81-107.

DATZ, Todd (2004): What You Need to Know About Service-Oriented Architecture, http://www.cio.com/archive/011504/soa.html, published: 15.01.2004, downloaded: 14.08.2005.

DOSTAL, Wolfgang / JECKLE, Mario / MELZER, Ingo / ZENGLER, Barbara (2005): Service-orientierte Architekturen mit Web Services, 1. Edition, München.

ERL, Thomas (2005): Core principles for service-oriented architectures, http://www.looselycoupled.com/opinion/2005/erl-core-infr0815.html, published: 15.08.2005, downloaded: 10.09.2005.

ESTREM, William A. (2003): An evaluation framework for developing Web Services in the next generation manufacturing enterprise, in: Robotic and Computer Integrated Manufacturing, December 2003, Vol. 19, Iss. 6, pp. 509-519.

FLEISHER, Craig S. / **BENSOUSSAN**, Babette E. (2003): Strategic and Competitive Intelligence, 1. Edition, Upper Saddle River.

FLOOD, Sally (2005): WHY STICK YOUR NECK OUT?, in: Computer Weekly, 5/17/2005, pp. 40-41.

GAINES, B. R. (1977): Hardware engineering and software engineering, in: Euromicro Newsletter, April 1977, Vol. 3, Iss. 2, pp. 16-21.

GARVER, Rob (2005): The Move Toward Service-Oriented Architectures, in: American Banker, July 2005, Vol. 170, Iss. 142, pp. 14ET-15ET.

GISOLFI, Dan (2001): Web services architect: Part 1 – An introduction to dynamic e-business, http://www-128.ibm.com/developerworks/webservices/library/ws-arc1/, published: 01.04.2001, downloaded: 08.09.2005.

GOLD-BERNSTEIN, Beth (2005): SOA Fundamentals, http://www.ebizq.net/hot_topics/soa/features/6245.html, published: 09.04.2005, downloaded: 05.09.2005.

GRUMAN, Galen (2005): SOA Ensures Guardian Gets It Right, in: InfoWorld, May 2005, Vol. 27, Iss. 18, pp. 63-64.

GUDGIN, Martin / HADLEY, Marc / MENDELSOHN, Noah / MOREAU, Jean-Jacques / FRYSTYK NIELSEN, Henrik (2003): SOAP Version 1.2 Part 1: Messaging Framework, http://www.w3.org/TR/soap12-part1/, published: 24.06.2003, downloaded: 16.09.2005.

HALL, Mark (2005): A Soft Touch, in: Computerworld, August 2005, Vol. 39, Iss. 33, p. 42.

HAVENSTEIN, Heather (2005): Adapting to SOA, in: Computerworld, August 2005, Vol. 39, Iss. 33, pp. 34-35.

HOLLIS, Emily (2005): Service-Oriented Architecture: It's Evolution, Baby, in: Certification Magazine, July 2005, Vol. 7, Iss. 7, p. 40.

HORSTMANN, Markus / **KIRTLAND**, Mary (1997): DCOM Architecture, http://msdn.microsoft.com/library/default.asp?url=/library/en-us/dndcom/html/msdn_dcomarch.asp, published: 23.07.1997, downloaded: 12.09.2005.

IBM (2005): Web Services – UDDI Business Registry, http://www-306.ibm.com/software/solutions/webservices/uddi/, published: n. a., downloaded: 16.09.2005.

INFOWORLD (2005): SOA Meets the Real World, in: InfoWorld, May 2005, Vol. 27, Iss. 18, pp. 58-59.

JURIC, Matjaz (2004): BPEL4WS, http://www.ebpml.org/bpel4ws.htm, published: 10.08.2004; downloaded: 19.09.2005.

KENDLER, Peggy Bresnick (2005): SOA: Plug and Play, in: Insurance & Technology, March 2005, Vol. 30, Iss. 3, pp. 40-41.

KERNER, Sean Michael (2004a): Web Services Market to Explode, http://www.internetnews.com/stats/article.php/3413161, published: 27.09.2004, downloaded: 14.09.2005.

KERNER, Sean Michael (2004b): SOA Investments on The Rise, Yankee Says, http://www.internetnews.com/ent-news/article.php/3416341, published: 01.10.2004, downloaded: 14.09.2005.

KHANNA, Poonam (2005): SOA plants the seeds of true system integration, in: Computing Canada, July 2005, Vol. 31, Iss. 10, p. 18.

KM WORLD (2005): Fuego and Proforma team up, in: KM World, July/August 2005, Vol. 14, Iss. 7, p. 30.

KOSCHEL, Arne / **STARKE**, Gernot (2005): Trends: Serviceorientierte Architekturen, in: Objektspectrum, 2005, Iss. 3, pp. 18-19.

KOSSMANN, Donal / **LEYMANN**, Frank (2004): Web Services, in: Informatik Spektrum, April 2004, pp. 117-128.

LUNDQUIST, Eric (2005): Simplicity isn't simple, in: eWeek, July 2005, Vol. 22, Iss. 28, p. 22.

MACVITTIE, Lori (2005): SOA Demystified, in: Network Computing, August 2005, Vol. 16, Iss. 15, pp. 77-80.

MANES, Anne Thomas (2005): THE ELEPHANT HAS LEFT THE BUILDING, in: Intelligent Enterprise, July 2005, Vol. 8, Iss. 7, pp. 22-29.

MANUFACTURING BUSINESS TECHNOLOGY (2005): SOA figures prominently in SAP transformation, in: Manufacturing Business Technology, July 2005, Vol. 23, Iss. 7, pp. 8-9.

MCKEAN, Kevin (2005a): Business-ification of IT, in: InfoWorld, May 2005, Vol. 27, Iss. 21, p. 8.

MCKEAN, Kevin (2005b): SOA's Tipping Point, in: InfoWorld, March 2005, Vol. 27, Iss. 10, p. 4.

MCKEAN, Kevin (2005c): Barriers to SOA Entry, in: InfoWorld, February 2005, Vol. 27, Iss. 6, p. 6.

MCKEAN, Kevin (2005d): Services at Your Service, in: InfoWorld, April 2005, Vol. 27, Iss. 17, p. 8.

MIHAJLOSKI, Kristian (2004): Web Service zur automatischen Softwareverteilung, Diplomarbeit, Kaiserslautern.

MOSCHELLA, David (2005): IP's Problem Is Too Many Dipsticks, in: Computerworld, August 2005, Vol. 39, Iss. 33, pp. 18-19.

NATIONAL MORTGAGE NEWS (2004): SOATech May Lead to Smooth M&A, in: National Mortgage News, December 2004, Vol. 29, Iss. 13, p. 6.

OMG (2004): Catalog Of OMG CORBA®/IIOP®Specification, http://www.omg.org/technology/documents/corba_spec_catalog.htm, published: 01.03.2004, downloaded: 15.09.2005.

PASLEY, James (2005): SOAs & ESBs, in: Dr. Dobb's Journal: Software Tools for the Professional Programmer, February 2005, Vol. 30, Iss. 2, pp. 24-29.

QUANTZ, Joachim / **WICHMANN**, Thorsten (2003): Basisreport Integration mit Web Services – Konzept, Fallstudien und Bewertung, http://www.berlecon.de/cgi/download.pl?file=200308BRWebServices.pdf&uid=&lang= Deutsch, published: 08.2003, downloaded: 15.09.2005.

ROBEY, Daniel / BOUDREAU, Marie-Claude / ROSE, Gregory M. (2000): Information technology and organizational learning: a review and assessment of research, in: Accounting, Management and Information Technologies, April 2000, Vol. 10, Iss. 2, pp. 125-155.

SILVER, Bruce (2005): Agile To the Bone, in: Intelligent Enterprise, February 2005, Vol. 8, Iss. 2, pp. 26-30.

SMITH, Mark (2005): Setting Priorities To Achieve Agility, in: Intelligent Enterprise, February 2005, Vol. 8, Iss. 2, p. 12.

SOMERS, Fergal (2005): ESB and BPEL: Changing the Rules of Integration, http://www.ebizq.net/topics/esb/features/5924.html, published: 15.05.2005, downloaded: 17.09.2005.

SUN (1997): Java™ Remote Method Invocation Specifiaction, http://java.sun.com/j2se/1.4.2/docs/guide/rmi/spec/rmi-title.html, published: 1997 (year of copyright), downloaded: 12.09.2005.

TAFT, Darryl K. (2004): Move over, EAI., in: eWeek, November 2004, Vol. 21, Iss. 47, p. 32.

TANNENBAUM, Andrew S. (2003): Computernetzwerke, 4. Auflage, München.

TILLER, Jim (2005): Digging Trenches, in: Information Systems Security, September /October 2005, Vol. 14, Iss. 4, pp. 2-4.

UDELL, Jon (2005a): Service-Oriented Architectures, in: InfoWorld, March 2005, Vol. 27, Iss. 11, pp. 48-49.

UDELL, Jon (2005b): Debugging SOA, in: InfoWorld, June 2005, Vol. 27, Iss. 23, p. 30.

VOELKER, Michael P. (2005): Plug and Play Meets Process, in: Intelligent Enterprise, February 2005, Vol. 8, Iss. 2, pp. 31-35.

WALLNAU, Kurt (1997): Software Technology Roadmap: Common Object Request Broker Architecture, http://www.sei.cmu.edu/str/descriptions/corba_body.html, published: 10.01.1997, downloaded: 14.09.2005.

WEBSTER, John S. (2005): Health Services, in: Computerworld, July 2005, Vol. 39, Iss. 30, pp. 26-28.

WIKIPEDIA (2005): Service-oriented architecture, http://en.wikipedia.org/wiki/Service-Oriented_Architecture, published: 2005 (year of last modification), downloaded: 08.09.2005.

WILKES, Lawrence (2003): SOA and web services, http://www.looselycoupled.com/opinion/2003/wilkes-soa-infr0415.html, published: 15.04.2003, downloaded: 09.09.2005.

WOLTER, Roger (2001): Simply SOAP, http://msdn.microsoft.com/library/default.asp?url=/library/en-us/dnexxml/html/Xml10152001.asp, published: 15.10.2001, downloaded: 14.09.2005.

YAGER, Tom (2004): Imagine No Possessions, in: InfoWorld, November 2004, Vol. 26, Iss. 47, p. 50.

YERGEAU, François / BRAY, Tim / PAOLI, Jean / SPERBERG-MCQUEEN, C. M. / MALER, Eve (2004): Extensible Markup Language (XML) 1.0 (Third Edition), http://www.w3.org/TR/REC-xml/, published: 04.02.2004, downloaded: 14.09.2005.

ZEICHNICK, Alan (2005): Desperately Seeking SOA, in: InfoWorld, January 2005, Vol. 27, Iss. 1, pp. 36-37.

ZIMMERMANN, Olaf / TOMLINSON, Mark / PEUSER, Stefan (2004): Perspectives on Web Services, 1. Edition, Berlin/Heidelberg.

YOUR KNOWLEDGE HAS VALUE

- We will publish your bachelor's and master's thesis, essays and papers

- Your own eBook and book - sold worldwide in all relevant shops

- Earn money with each sale

Upload your text at www.GRIN.com
and publish for free

www.ingramcontent.com/pod-product-compliance
Lightning Source LLC
LaVergne TN
LVHW042300060326
832902LV00009B/1157